9/11

Drawing Is Fun!

DRAWING
FANTASY FIGURES

Gareth Stevens
Publishing

Please visit our Web site, www.garethstevens.com. For a free color catalog of all our high-quality books, call toll free 1-800-542-2595 or fax 1-877-542-2596.

Library of Congress Cataloging-in-Publication Data

Cook, Trevor, 1948-
Drawing fantasy figures / Trevor Cook and Lisa Miles.
    p. cm. — (Drawing is fun!)
Includes index.
ISBN 978-1-4339-5065-0 (pbk.)
ISBN 978-1-4339-5066-7 (6-pack)
ISBN 978-1-4339-5022-3 (library binding)
1. Fantasy in art—Juvenile literature. 2. Drawing—Technique—Juvenile literature. I. Miles, Lisa. II. Title.
NC1764.8.F37C66 2011
743'.87—dc22

                           2010027758

First Edition

Published in 2011 by
Gareth Stevens Publishing
111 East 14th Street, Suite 349
New York, NY 10003

Copyright © 2011 Arcturus Publishing

Artwork: Q2A India
Text: Trevor Cook and Lisa Miles
Editors: Fiona Tulloch and Joe Harris
Cover design: Akihiro Nakayama

Picture credits: All photographs supplied by Shutterstock, except page 12:
Mark Kolbe/Getty Images.

Printed in the United States

CPSIA compliance information: Batch #AW11GS: For further information contact Gareth Stevens, New York, New York at 1-800-542-2595.

SL001770US

Contents

Fairy

In stories, a fairy is a magical creature.

Fairies can fly. This one has wings like a butterfly.

Fairies are helpful and kind to people.

She looks like a person, only she is very tiny.

FUN FACTS ● FUN FACTS ● FUN FACTS ● FUN FACTS ● FUN FACTS

In books and movies, one of the most famous fairies is Tinker Bell. She is the friend of Peter Pan.

1. Start with the slim body.

2. Now draw her head and her hair.

3. Put in her arms and her legs.

4. Add the wings so she can fly!

Superhero

Superheroes have amazing powers. Some can fly.

Superheroes help people who are in danger.

Many superheroes wear capes.

Superheroes are very strong. Some are so strong they can lift a car!

FUN FACTS ● FUN FACTS ● FUN FACTS ● FUN FACTS ● FUN FACTS

The most famous superhero of all is called Superman. The first Superman comic book was in 1938.

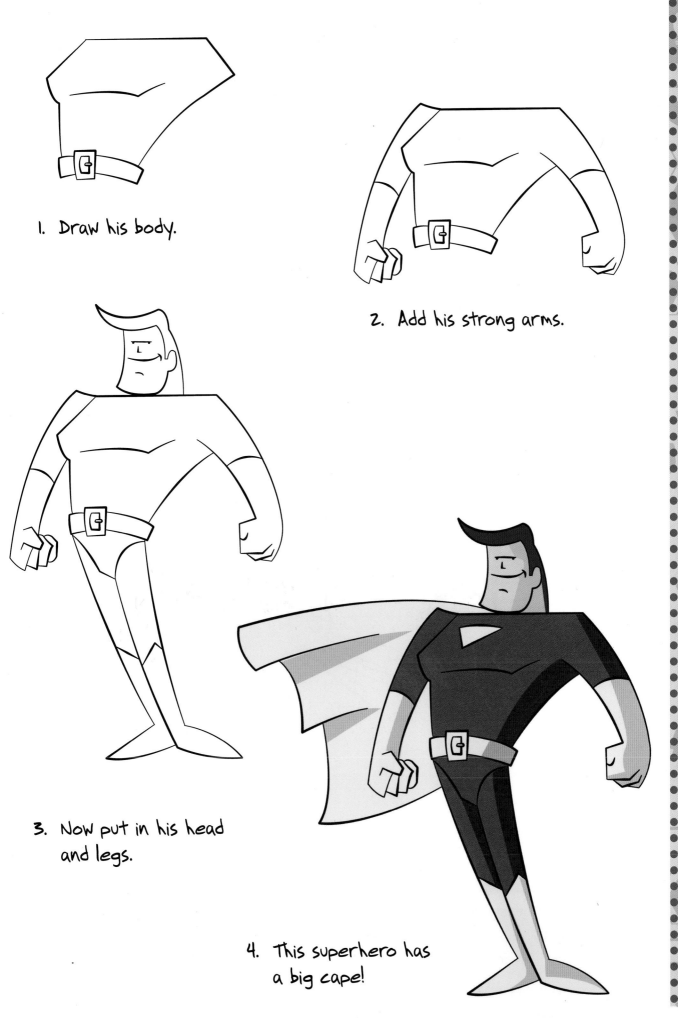

1. Draw his body.

2. Add his strong arms.

3. Now put in his head and legs.

4. This superhero has a big cape!

Wizard

This wizard is old and wise. He has a long beard.

He is wearing a pointed hat. It has a moon and a star on it.

He carries a magic stick called a staff.

He wears a long cape.

FUN FACTS ● FUN FACTS ● FUN FACTS ● FUN FACTS ● FUN FACTS

Not all wizards are old. One of the most famous wizards is a schoolboy called Harry Potter!

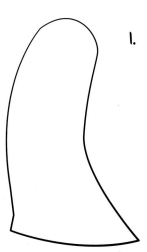

1. Draw the body first.

2. Now put in his pointy hat and his pointy beard.

3. Finish his face and draw in his arms.

4. In his hand he's holding his magic staff.

Dragon

A dragon is a huge monster that can fly.

It has a neck like a snake.

It can breathe fire! It uses the fire to scare people away.

It has a body like a huge lizard. It also has big wings.

FUN FACTS • FUN FACTS • FUN FACTS • FUN FACTS • FUN FACTS

In many stories, dragons are bad. However in China, dragons are meant to bring happiness and good luck!

1. Draw a snaky body shape.

2. Put in the spiky head.

3. He has four legs.

4. His wings are out. He's breathing fire!

Mermaid

In stories, a mermaid is is half human and half fish.

She has long hair. Mermaids often carry a comb and a mirror.

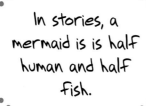

She has a girl's body and a fish's tail.

A creature with a man's body and a fish's tail is called a merman.

FUN FACTS ● FUN FACTS ● FUN FACTS ● FUN FACTS ● FUN FACTS

Long ago, sailors told stories about mermaids who sang to them. Sailors thought mermaids were bad luck!

1. Here's her body.

2. Draw her long hair and her fishy tail.

3. Add her face and arms.

4. Put in some bubbles so we can see she's in the water.

Witch

A scary woman who does magic is called a witch.

She wears a pointy witch's hat.

She has a tooth missing and a wart on her nose.

She is wearing a long black dress. She has green skin!

FUN FACTS ● FUN FACTS ● FUN FACTS ● FUN FACTS ● FUN FACTS

Long ago, people thought that witches were real. If they got sick, they might think it was a witch's magic spell!

1. Here's her body.

2. Draw her head and tall hat.

3. She has long messy hair.

4. She's riding through the air on a broomstick!

Pirate

Pirates sail across the sea in pirate ships. They steal from other ships.

This pirate has a big, black pirate hat.

A pirate needs to be good at sailing and fighting.

Many pirates were injured in fights.

FUN FACTS ● FUN FACTS ● FUN FACTS ● FUN FACTS ● FUN FACTS

Pirate ships flew a flag called the Jolly Roger. It showed a picture of a skull with two crossed bones!

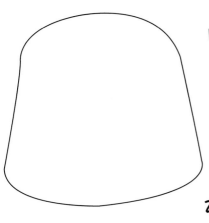

1. His body is shaped like a barrel.

2. On top you can draw his hat.

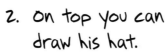

3. The best pirates have eyepatches.

4. He's got one eye, one hand and one leg. Yo ho ho!

Zombie

In stories, a zombie is a dead person who has come back to life.

He walks in a stiff, clumsy way.

He is scary. He likes to eat people!

Zombies follow each other in a big group. They don't think for themselves.

FUN FACTS ● FUN FACTS ● FUN FACTS ● FUN FACTS ● FUN FACTS

In stories, zombies are brought to life by a bad wizard. He controls what they do!

1. This shape has lots of corners.

2. Put in the strange stiff arms.

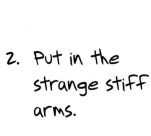

3. His legs are bendy.

4. He looks very cross.

Queen

A queen is a woman who rules a country.

The queen is rich. She wears lots of jewels.

She looks very important. She tells people what to do!

She wears a dress that costs a lot of money.

FUN FACTS ● FUN FACTS ● FUN FACTS ● FUN FACTS ● FUN FACTS

One famous queen from history was Elizabeth I of England. She was very powerful and never got married!

1. She has a very curvy body.

2. Draw her puff sleeves and big skirt.

3. Give her a little crown, but a huge collar.

4. In her hands she's holding a scepter.

Mummy

In ancient Egypt, people wrapped dead bodies up in bandages.

In stories and movies, sometimes a mummy comes back to life. He scares people!

The bodies are called mummies.

Some stories say that a person who finds a mummy will have bad luck.

FUN FACTS ● FUN FACTS ● FUN FACTS ● FUN FACTS ● FUN FACTS

In Egypt, scientists uncover mummies that have been buried for thousands of years!

1. Draw his head and rectangular body.

2. Give him staring eyes and make his hands reach out.

3. He's jumping at us!

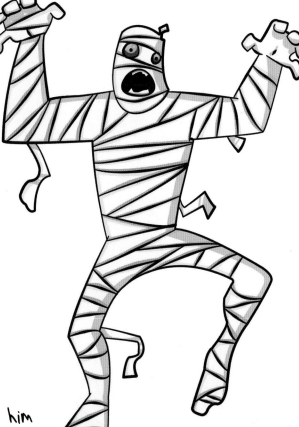

4. Cover him in bandages. Give him green eyes.

Vampire

In stories, a vampire is a creature that drinks people's blood!

He likes to wear black clothes.

He only comes out at night. He is scared of daylight.

If someone is bitten by a vampire, they turn into a vampire too!

FUN FACTS ● FUN FACTS ● FUN FACTS ● FUN FACTS ● FUN FACTS

A famous vampire from books and movies is Count Dracula. He can turn into a bat or a mist.

1. Start with these two shapes.

2. Draw staring eyes and curly fingers.

3. His cape swirls around him.

4. Put two sharp fangs in his mouth.

Giant

Giants are big but they are not very smart.

They sometimes try to eat people.

Giants like fighting. This one is carrying a huge club.

He has a necklace made of bones.

FUN FACTS ● FUN FACTS ● FUN FACTS ● FUN FACTS ● FUN FACTS

There is a giant in the story of Jack and the Beanstalk. The giant lives in a castle on a cloud.

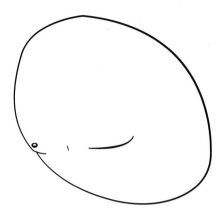

1. Draw a big, round body.

2. Add the head and legs.

3. Put in the arms and the big club.

4. Color the club like a piece of wood.

Alien

An alien is a creature from another planet.

The alien looks like a bit like a person. It has big eyes and a thin body.

If aliens exist, some people think they might look like this.

An alien could look like anything at all. You can use your imagination!

FUN FACTS ● FUN FACTS ● FUN FACTS ● FUN FACTS ● FUN FACTS

Scientists are always looking for signs of alien life in space. But so far, they haven't found any!

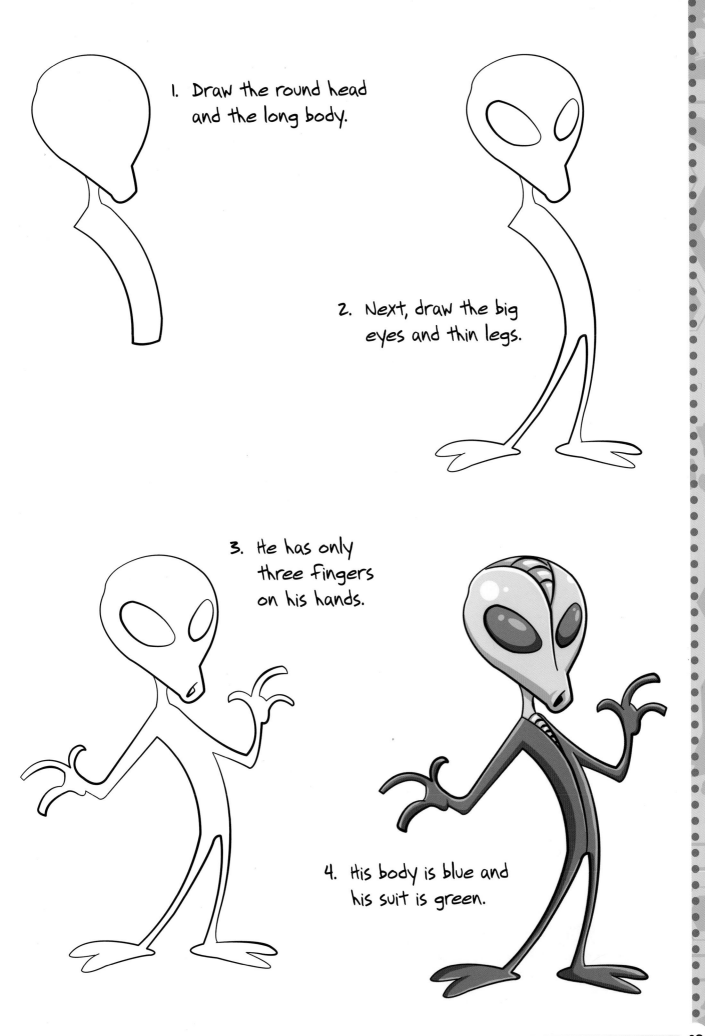

1. Draw the round head and the long body.

2. Next, draw the big eyes and thin legs.

3. He has only three fingers on his hands.

4. His body is blue and his suit is green.

Troll

A troll is a horrible, ugly monster.

This troll has a big club.

Trolls never wash. They smell really bad.

Trolls sometimes live under bridges.

FUN FACTS ● FUN FACTS ● FUN FACTS ● FUN FACTS ● FUN FACTS

In some stories, trolls are scared of sunlight. If they go out in sunlight, they turn to stone!

1. Draw a big, wide body.

2. Give him sharp teeth and ears.

3. He has two small legs.

4. In his hand he carries a club with nails in it.

Glossary

bandages long pieces of cloth. These are sometimes wrapped around someone who has been badly hurt.

broomstick a stick for brushing away dust and dirt

cape a piece of clothing that is worn over your shoulders and back

collar part of a piece of clothing that goes around your neck

comb this is used to tidy hair

clumsy likely to fall or knock things over

comic book a book with pictures and speech bubbles. Some comic books are about superheroes.

creature an animal or person

eyepatch this covers someone's eye, or the place where their eye used to be

fang a sharp tooth

injure hurt badly

jewel a beautiful stone. Jewels cost a lot of money.

sailor someone who travels across the sea

scepter a rod with jewels on it. Kings and queens sometimes carry these.

slim thin

stiff hard to bend

wart a small, hard bump on someone's skin

Index

Further Reading

Colclough, V. Shane. *Fantastic Realms! Draw Fantasy Characters, Creatures and Settings*. Impact, 2006.

Hart, Christopher. *How to Draw Fantasy Characters*. Watson-Guptill, 1999.

Renaigle, Damon J. *Draw Medieval Fantasies*. Peel Productions, 1995.